Who I am

Sophie Martin

BookLeaf Publishing

India | USA | UK

Presentation by *BookLeaf Publishing*

Web: www.bookleafpub.com

E-mail: info@bookleafpub.com

ISBN: 9789360945077

First edition 2024

I dedicate this book to all those I have along my journey of discovery. To those I met in recovery, you all know who you are, your spirit, unwavering honesty, unconditional love, support and grace will be with me forever.

To my Krav family, thank you for pushing me to my limits, for making me work hard, supporting me when I think I can do no more and for celebrating the victories alongside me. Krav Maga changed my life and I am grateful for everyone that I have met on my Krav Maga journey.

To my family. There are no words. No words to say how much I love you. All I can ever do is try to show you all each day what you mean to me. For everything that you have given me, from the bottom of my heart thank you.

To my children - all of you - you drive me bonkers but I love seeing you grow, smile, giggle and change. Forever be true to you, chase knowledge and continue to love, respect and show kindness to all. I love you more than there are stars in the universe.

John, my husband, my soul mate. Thank you for loving me for me. For never wanting me to change, for believing in me and for accepting me. Thank you for choosing me and for opening your heart up to me.

I

1

I am a mother.
I am a wife.
I am a sister.
I am an employer.

I am 5'5.
I am a brunette.
I am a glasses wearer.
I am brown eyed.

Who am I?

Choices

Choices

I made a choice three times prior;
Choices that changed my life forever;
Enriched my soul and made me put three
choices first.

I made a choice once prior;
A choice that changed my life forever;
This choice enriched my soul three times over.

I am not your mother nor will I ever be;
But I will always be here to dry your tears;
I will always be there to hold your hand;
I will always celebrate your wins and support
your losses.

You make me cry and sigh;
But you make me laugh and smile.

I may not be your mother;
But I am glad I chose you.

10 Hours

Tick
Smells of cleaning fluid fill my brain
I feel optimistic walking in, filled with hope that
this will be over soon
I see an army of people waiting
Some crying; some sleeping
It's then I realise that it's desperation in the air

Tick tock
I hear my name called and I jump up as best as I
can
Maybe this will be over soon.
I answer there questions;
I pee in a cup;
And I return to my seat.

Tick tock; tick
The seat I am in touches my hips;
I can't get comfortable.
My person leaves and I am alone.
I ask when it's me.
I want to leave.
My body hurts from the chair.
It hurts to breathe.

Tick tock; tick tock
I hear my name and I rush to be seen.
This will all be over soon.
I can go back to my bed.
I answer their questions yet again.
It could be serious they say
Do not leave

Tick tock; tick tock; tick
I see people leaving
I see people coming
I see people pacing
I sit and I wait.
I shuffle to get comfortable.
I want to sleep.
But I don't want to miss my name

Tick tock; tick tock; tick tock
I hear them call me again.
I go for their tests.
I return and I am back to the familiar see of
faces.
The murmuring sounds like thunder in my ears.
I try to listen in to conversations but I can't
People comparing their waiting time.
Hopelessness overcomes me.

Tock tock; tick tock; tick tock; tick

I hear my name again and I don't bother to get
excited anymore.
My tests were fine.
I can leave.
I walk out and I don't look back.
Fresh air engulfs me bringing me back to life.

Tick tock; tick tock; tick tock; tick tock;
I sink in to my sofa.
I smell my living room; the faint waft of incense
washing over me.
I can finally rest.

Love/Hate/Shame

Don't leave me
Leave me
Get out
I hate you
Please stay

You never listen to me leave me alone I hate you
I don't hate you I hate me more please come
back I miss you I didn't mean it I can't breathe
it's too much there's too much going on I can't
work it out I'm so angry I am so sad every part
of me is hurting and I don't know how to deal
but I just want to feel something please don't
leave I couldn't take it without you I hate myself
you deserve more you deserve better I mean it
you deserve the world and I can't give it to you
why do I do this why can't I stop I am not
worthy I just can't do it anymore

I

Just

Can't

Do

It

Anymore

Love is

Love is making me feel unequivocally beautiful
Beautiful mind
Beautiful soul
Beautiful body

Love is listening to my stories
Long stories
Boring stories
Funny stories

Love is embracing my scars
Emotional scars
Physical scars
Mental scars

Love is giving me space to cry
Cry from laughter
Cry from sorrow
Cry from happiness

Love is dancing
Dancing in the kitchen
Dancing in the streets
Dancing wherever life takes us

Love is lifting me up
Lifting me up when I'm down
Lifting me up when I fall
Lifting me up just because you can

Love is truth
Even when I'm being an arse
Even when I should apologise
Even on the occasion that I am right

Love is vulnerability
Even when it's scary
Even when it's exposing
Even when it's raw

Love is being able to hold you in the dark
Love is being able to celebrate with you in the
light
Love is the the joy of knowing you for you and
me for me

I Give

I give to you

My heart
My smelly feet

My soul
My clutter

My truth
My ditzyness

My giggles
My shoes

My hugs
My snores

My kisses
My floordrobe

My all

Bleed

The blade held against the skin
Slowly drawing back
The feel of skin breaking
Pressure releasing
Blood pouring
The relief instantaneous
Frantic slashing to keep the release
For a brief moment I feel free and then

Shame

My Eldest

12

You gave meaning to my world
Made my blacks and whites turn to glorious
technicolour
The pride I have for the person that you are
cannot be explained
You gave me the greatest job I could ever have
asked for.
You will forever be my first born.
I love you.

Middle

13

You are kind
You are funny
You are sweet
You are cheeky
You are the reason my eyebrow raises so high
You are the reason I laugh until I cry
No day is the same with you
I am forever grateful for you
You have the innocence of a young child on the
cusp of discovering the cruel realities of the
world.
Never forget I am always here to to dull the
harshness and make you smile.

I love you

Littlest

You may be the littlest but you have huge heart
You still love mummy hugs and cuddles
You have the innocence of youth that believes in
all of the magical things in the world.
Father Christmas. The Easter Bunny and The
Tooth Fairy.
I hope that you never change but I know that one
day you will be grown ....
I will miss these days and cherish them forever
more but I cannot wait to see you flourish in to
an incredible young woman.
I love you.

Happiness

I used to think that happiness and success meant
fast cars.
That a skinny body and a big bank account
meant I would be happy.
I thought a fancy house would make a home.
I thought flash holidays meant that everyone
wanted what I had.
Manicures, hair styles and fancy clothes.
This is what I was told was success.

Yet despite the shiny exterior I drank away my
shame, my poor self esteem and my self hatred.

My happiness is waking up next to him.
Wild camping with the family
Movie nights
Our first holiday together watching as you swim
in the ocean
Exploring new cities
Getting lost in the woods
Training
Long walks whilst the rain beats down
Going to the beach and eating sandwiches that
we brought from home.
Incense burning and the fire roaring

Geocaching
Firework displays followed by hot chocolate

This is my true happiness….
This is makes me feel whole.

Time

Time disappears so quickly
Sometime the moments and times that we should
enjoy are mere flickers
Work and housework
Take those moments from us before we even
realised we should cherish them.
Sometimes it's important to stop. Breathe.
Forget the washing
Forget the dishes
Dance like no one is watching
Hold those that you cherish
Smell they're skin and their shampoo
Cuddle them.
Swing them round
Sing as though no one is listening
Don't let time disappear
Stop time
Appreciate it
For when it is gone it can never be reclaimed

5,4,3,2,1

5 things I can see
4 things I can hear
3 things I can smell
2 things I can touch
1 thing I can taste

Has saved my life over and over

Imposter

I don't belong here
I'm not good enough
I will never be good enough
I am not smart enough
I am not pretty enough
I am not deserving enough
I will let you down
I shouldn't be doing this
I don't feel right

Then I smile to save from crying
And I pull up my big girl pants
And I smile and start another day.

No

Is a full sentence.

You're

My fuckwit

Emotions

I feel pain like it's dagger in me chest
I feel sorrow like I've had the world ripped from
me
I feel joy like the world is made of unicorns
I fear abandonment when there's nothing to fear;
so crippling I push those I love away.
I feel nerves so I shake
Anxiety like I can't breathe

I feel things a million times harder then most
And I have to take pills to control it and will
forever more
This is a part of me
But this does not define me

Me

I love the warmth of the sun on my skin
I love cheese
I am introverted
Unless you really know me and then you can't
stop me
I am fierce and yet timid
I am generous and yet selfish
I am patient and yet once my tolerance has been
pushed I am unforgiving.
I will do anything for you until you piss me off
and then I am over you.
Spiders scare me… but only the big ones
I love swimming in the ocean but not too far out
…there's sharks
I love sleep
I love bed
I am tactile and need to have physical touch
But not strangers … don't touch me
I need reassurance but when I have it I am
independent
I need to feel safe
I am chronically insecure
I suffer with terrible imposter syndrome
The slightest criticism can feel like I've been
wiped out

I am stubborn.
I am passionate.
I am kind.
I am honest.
I am sober.

I am not my labels.

9 789360 945077